GW01220395

Table of Contents

The ultimate guide to the law of attraction for beginners

What Is the Law of Attraction?

The law of attraction is the New Thought spiritual belief that positive or negative thoughts bring positive or negative experiences into a person's life.

The belief is based on the idea that people and their thoughts are made from "pure energy" and that like energy can attract like energy, thereby allowing people to improve their health, wealth, or personal relationships.

There is no empirical scientific evidence supporting the law of attraction, and it is widely considered to be pseudoscience.

Advocates generally combine cognitive reframing techniques with affirmations and creative visualization to replace limiting or self-destructive ("negative") thoughts with more empowered, adaptive ("positive") thoughts.

A key component of the philosophy is the idea that in order to effectively change one's negative thinking patterns, one must also "feel" (through creative visualization) that the desired changes have already occurred.

This combination of positive thought and positive emotion is believed to allow one to attract positive experiences and opportunities by achieving resonance with the proposed energetic law.

Supporters of the law of attraction refer to scientific theories and use them as arguments in favor of it. However, it has no demonstrable scientific basis.A number of researchers have criticized the misuse of scientific concepts by its proponents.

How Your Thoughts Can Influence Outcomes in Your Life

The law of attraction is a philosophy suggesting that positive thoughts bring positive results into a person's life, while negative thoughts bring negative outcomes. It is based on the belief that thoughts are a form of energy and that positive energy attracts success in all areas of life, including health, finances, and relationships.

Based on these lofty promises, it begs the question: Is the law of attraction real? While the law of attraction has generated attention in recent years due to books like "The Secret," it lacks scientific evidence for its claims and is generally viewed as a pseudoscience.

The Laws of Attraction

How does the law of attraction work? Essentially, the energy of your thoughts manifest your experiences. So positive thoughts manifest positive experiences and vice versa. Advocates suggest there are central universal principles that make up the law of attraction:

- **Like attracts like:** This law suggests that similar things are attracted to one another. It means that people tend to attract people who are similar to them—but it also suggests that people's thoughts tend to attract similar results. Negative thinking is believed to attract negative experiences, while positive thinking is believed to produce desirable experiences.

- **Nature abhors a vacuum:** This law of attraction suggests that removing negative things from your life can make space for more positive things to take their place. It is based on the notion that it is impossible to have a completely empty space in your mind and in your life. Since something will always fill this space, it is important to fill that space with positivity, proponents of this philosophy say.

- **The present is always perfect:** This law focuses on the idea that there are always things you can do to improve the present moment. While it might always seem like the present is somehow flawed, this law proposes that, rather than feeling dread or unhappiness, you should focus your energy on finding ways to make the present moment the best that it can be.

How to Use the Law of Attraction

So how do you get started with the law of attraction? According to this philosophy, you create your own reality. What you focus on is what you draw into your life. It suggests that what you believe will happen in your life is what does happen.

Some things that you can do to incorporate the law of attraction into your own life include:

- Be grateful
- Visualize your goals
- Look for the positives in a situation
- Learn how to identify negative thinking
- Use positive affirmations
- Reframe negative events in a more positive way

While the law of attraction may not be an immediate solution for all of life's challenges, it can help you learn to cultivate a more optimistic outlook on life. It may also help you stay motivated to continue working toward your goals.

Relationships

You can use some elements of the law of attraction to work toward your relationship goals. One way to do this is to become more aware of the things that might be holding you back when it comes to allowing love in your life.

If you notice that issues like a fear of vulnerability keep you from forging strong romantic connections, you can start taking steps to overcome those fears. Approaching your relationships with positivity may help you form healthier relationships.

Work

The law of attraction can also be useful for achieving your professional goals. While people sometimes mistakenly believe that simply thinking positively about your career aspirations will manifest positive changes, the key is to use your long-term goals to make specific, concrete changes in the present that will help you take steps toward your goals.

For example, simply hoping for higher pay isn't enough. Taking actions such as acquiring marketable skills, seeking promotions, or even pursuing a new position are steps you can take that will pay off in the future. According to the law of attraction, focusing your energy in positive ways will bring positive changes to your life in the future.

Money

Manifesting financial changes in your life requires small steps and steady progress. Instead of simply wishing for more, it's important to assess your financial life and set goals for what you want to achieve both now and in the future.

The law of attraction encourages people to shift from a scarcity mindset to an abundance mindset. Instead of focusing on what you lack, practice feeling gratitude for what you have. In doing so, you'll be better prepared as you work toward your financial goals and take advantage of the opportunities presented.

Impact of the Law of Attraction

While the law of attraction lacks scientific support, proponents suggest that it can produce positive changes in a person's life. Some reasons why people may experience benefits from this philosophy include:

- Spiritual Effects
- Better Well-Being

Tips for Practicing the Law of Attraction

There are some exercises that can help you learn to put the law of attraction into practice in your own life. Some ideas include:

- **Journaling:** Writing down your thoughts can help you better learn to recognize your habitual thought patterns to see whether you tend toward optimism or pessimism and learn more about changing negative patterns of thought.

- **Make a mood board:** Create a visual reminder that helps you maintain a positive mindset, stay motivated, and focus on your goals.

- **Practice acceptance:** Instead of focusing on what is wrong about the present or what needs to be changed, work on accepting things as they are. This doesn't mean that you won't continue to work toward a better future, it just means that you won't get bogged down by wishing for things to be different right now.

- **Practice positive self-talk:** If you struggle with being overly self-critical, set a goal to engage in positive self-talk each day. Over time, this may come much more easily and you may find that it is harder to maintain a negative mindset.

Do we attract what we think? It's a little more complicated but mindset matters

"There's no place like home. There's no place like home." Fans of The Wizard of Oz may appreciate Dorothy's efforts to will herself home, even if they've never heard of the law of attraction.

Dorothy does eventually get home, but, as we know in the movie and in real life, achieving our goals takes more than even the most heartfelt determination. It definitely takes more than repetition, the right shoes, and a few heel clicks.

Still, an optimistic mindset matters and we should take the power of positive thinking seriously.

Your thoughts have an impact on your life. Your mindset shapes your thoughts, behaviors, and actions. Behaviors tend to influence enters our lives and who stays, as a resource or a liability. Your thoughts and behaviors also shape how you feel about yourself and the world.

Fuelling your mind with negative thinking doesn't help your well-being or encourage flourishing, happy relationships. And it certainly doesn't help you manifest something better.

On some days, it's hard to look on the bright side. No one should expect to always feel or be positive but a positive attitude helps. So does an optimistic mindset. Changing the way you feel about yourself and the world can change the way people think about and treat you. That can have real outcomes.

This is the essence of harnessing "the law of attraction" to change your life. Why not start learning today?

This same law of attraction is really what?

Let's be upfront about this: The law of attraction isn't a law in the scientific or legal sense. There's currently no scientific evidence to back it up. It's one of several manifestation methods that argues that your thoughts impact your reality.

It suggests that someone who focuses too much on bad things will have negative experiences. But if someone hones their thoughts and subconscious mind into thinking about positive affirmations, more good things will happen.

With that said, the law of attraction uses strategies supported by evidence. These strategies include positive self-talk, visualization, and changing our biases to create a world we want to live in.

Positive thinking is linked to better physical health, longer life, and even a lower risk of heart disease. Research shows that keeping a growth mindset has mental health benefits, too. It can reduce stress, risk of depression, and aid in stress management.

This improved emotional state keeps you on track to build more skills, which will ultimately lead to greater success. And you'll even see increased mindfulness, gratitude, and self-compassion.

So what is the law of attraction? It states that whatever you focus your energy on will come back to you. By focusing on what you want to achieve, the law states that you'll emit positive energy to attract those achievements to you.

The law of attraction is treated as a natural law by self-help and self-care advocates, but we can thank the power of a positive attitude and an optimistic mindset.

A positive attitude doesn't mean relentless or toxic positivity. There's space to acknowledge reality, and reality doesn't always go our way every day. We have setbacks. We can rise above setbacks. In the same way, an optimistic mindset isn't about believing that "everything will just work out" if you believe hard enough.

An optimistic mindset is a belief that there is a solution or a way to resolve a problem or challenge. It's hope combined with action.

How does the law of attraction work?

How the law of attraction works can differ depending on who you talk to but it has several foundational behaviors. The first is a mindset, and the second is action. Some theories claim that you create a pull between you and what you desire in life when you focus intently.

But really, we make that happen through growth and action, not wishful thinking. You must bring your whole self to everything you do, professionally and personally. Our mental fitness\demands us to set goals, create a routine, and go on a journey of self-discovery.

That's where the growth mindset comes in. Your outlook on the world can shape many aspects of your life. Actively looking for the positive side of an issue helps us grow our self-esteem, and confidence and become better leaders. We can throw away our toxic traits and be brave and open to new opportunities.

That positive energy is infectious, too. Being open-minded and focusing on positive emotions attracts others who feel the same way. It helps entrepreneurs adopt an entrepreneurial mindset that helps them with their professional careers.

But for everyone, it helps us connect with people who share the same passion and goal of being authentically themselves.

BetterUp can guide you to develop a growth mindset full of grit, courage, and playfulness. Our coaches can provide the perspective and accountability you need to show up with positive energy and go-getter behavior.

What are the 7 laws of attraction?

Now to make things more confusing, when people talk about the law of attraction, they're actually referring to seven sub-laws. While we don't subscribe to any of these being natural laws, there are some worthwhile nuggets. See what you can find here in the seven laws of attraction:

1. Similar things are attracted to each other

This law explains that like attract likes. Negative thoughts attract one another, but positive thoughts do the same. If all we do is dwell on the negative, negative experiences that come our way. But if we seek out the positive aspects of life, our well-being will be more focused on finding good opportunities and experiences.

2. Focus on the present

We should already live in the present, but this law explains that we should focus our efforts on our current situation. If we put in the work now, our futures will be more positive and full of opportunities. Worrying about the future won't help us, either.

3. Make room for the positive things in life

Some negative things in our lives can be removed or changed. Toxic workplaces, relationships that don't fulfill you, or a career that doesn't satisfy you can prevent you from living a meaningful life.

By removing those negatives, we can replace them with more things that help us be more purposeful with our lives. Having a clear idea of your purpose and personal values can help guide you to things that enrich your life.

4. Find balance

Some days might not go the way you wanted. You might fail. Here's the thing: That's part of life. It's good to acknowledge our failures because they're an opportunity to learn. Just as we celebrate our wins, we can recognize our losses.

5. Remain unwavering in our desires

This law is all about staying focused on the goals and desires that will improve our lives. Clear, purposeful goals help us gain better health, succeed in our careers, and have healthy relationships.

Throughout the stages of our lives, we can experience many changes. But we need to know how we feel about our values and desires to stay grounded. And while our values or desires might evolve over our lives, having a clear sense of self will help us commit to our most important goals.

6. Create harmony around us

The harmony that we have around us can influence our energy. Tapping into the energy that surrounds us can help us as we try to stay positive while working toward our goals. When we have people around us that share the same mentality toward achieving goals, it only benefits us. They're a source of encouragement, support, and inspiration.

7. What goes around comes around

This law discusses that our actions affect everything and everyone around us. How we treat others has a direct impact on our lives. You could be an incredibly positive and hard-working person, but you likely aren't living meaningfully if you don't treat others with respect. And this will attract negative energy to you.

Choosing to offer a helping hand can go a long way, even if you don't think it directly benefits your life.

Utilizing the law of attraction to reach your goals

We can't promise that manifesting will help you reach your goals. But some of the tenets of the law of attraction can't hurt to try. Here's how to use the law of attraction in seven ways to achieve your goals:

1. Understand burnout and how to recover from it
2. Incorporate more positive affirmations and self-talk into your inner dialogue
3. Look for the positives, no matter how big or small, in every situation you're in
4. Practice visualization by keeping a manifestation journal or creating a vision board
5. Look for coincidences and patterns
6. Learn how to identify when you start thinking negative thoughts
7. Practice journaling your ideas, values, and plans

The disadvantages of the law of attraction

The law of attraction doesn't work for everybody. Without the proper understanding of this concept, people may think that simply being optimistic will reward them. Some people fall into a kind of magical thinking. But in truth, discipline and clear objectives are what reward us.

While it may be true that you can achieve anything you put your mind to, that only works if you quickly follow your mind with some sweat and hard work. Intentional, effective effort makes a difference on the road to our goals.

So does a little luck or serendipity. And perseverance has to keep you going when nothing else is going your way.

It's not magic.

Thinking positively but procrastinating on our actions won't bring us anywhere. But now you know that a positive viewpoint can inspire and drive us to work harder to reach our goals. The right attitude is one thing, but our behavior is what creates change.

We won't achieve much without motivation, resilience, courage, and grit. When we lack those characteristics but still want to harness the law of attraction, we may become disappointed and lose confidence in ourselves.

5 reasons why the law of attraction might not work

The law of attraction isn't a fool-proof way of achieving your goals and living your dream life. If you find that it isn't working out as you'd hoped, take a moment to reflect on your actions. Think about your behavior and how you're viewing the law of attraction.

Here are five reasons that the law of attraction might not be working for you at the moment:

1. You lack objectives and a purpose

2. You don't have any solid goals you want to achieve

3. You haven't been putting in the effort and hard work

4. Your self-esteem and self-confidence are poor

5. You're experiencing a lot of mental fatigue and stress, so you lack the necessary energy

It's not magic: it's attraction and action

Like many other aspects of your life, your dreams don't work unless you do. It's one thing to have a positive outlook on life, but that isn't what takes you places. And that's not what the law of attraction is.

It's all about the combination of action, planning, and positive thinking. The sustained efforts that you put into yourself now will benefit you in the future. And one day, you'll see for yourself what your positive and action-filled behavior has attracted you.

If you need extra help with balancing a positive attitude and sustained purposeful action, Better Up can help you. Our coaches will work with you to stay focused on your most ambitious goals.

A Complete Guide to Using the Law of Attraction

At this very moment, your life is being guided and influenced by universal forces you may not even be aware of – and the most powerful of all is the Law of Attraction. Just like the law of gravity, it is always in effect, impacting your life in more ways than you can imagine.

The good news is, once you are aware of this universal law, you can learn how to use it to change your life for the better! Because here's the thing: You are in a constant state of creation.

Every moment of every day, you are actively creating your reality. With every thought, either consciously or subconsciously, you are creating your future. And when you know how to harness the power of the Law of Attraction in your life, you can direct your thoughts and actions in a way that allows you to effortlessly attract what you want.

You may be thinking right now, "Wait a minute...The Law of Attraction is real?"

Many people, when they first hear about this universal law, dismiss it as "woo." So if you have doubts about whether it really works, you're certainly not alone! I often get questions from people who wonder what the Law of Attraction is and are skeptical about the claims they've heard. And I'm going to tell you what I always tell them:

Expect miracles.

When you understand how the Law of Attraction works, you can use it to change your life for the better and create an amazing future.

This guide will walk you through the process of using this powerful universal law and show you how to manifest what you want in every area of your life. I'll teach you about the 7 Laws of Attraction (that's right, there are more than one) and the 3 proven steps to activate it in your life. You'll also learn how to use it for different purposes, such as attracting more wealth or love into your life.

Buckle up, because it's going to be an amazing ride

Why Does the Universe Use the Law of Attraction?

Simply put, it's because like attracts like. If you are feeling excited, enthusiastic, passionate, happy, joyful, appreciative, or abundant, then you are sending out positive energy to the universe.

In turn, that positive energy will attract people, resources, and opportunities that resonate on the same energetic wavelength. This optimism that is effortlessly brought into your path of life will allow you to reach your goals.

On the other hand, if you are feeling bored, anxious, stressed out, angry, resentful, or sad, you are sending out negative energy. That negative energy will repel positivity and attract pessimistic people and events into your life.

Discovering the Law of Attraction in Your Life

You have probably noticed the law of attraction in your own life. For example, a person who complains all the time typically attracts friends or followers who also have a bad attitude. Or happy and energetic people will attract other motivated go-getters into their circle.

That's the Universal Law of Attraction in action!

It's important to note that the Universe doesn't care what kind of energetic vibration you send out. It doesn't "care" if you are a positive or negative person. It simply responds to what you offer.

By changing your energetic vibration, you can change the way the universe responds to you! You can manifest particular outcomes in your life simply by creating and leaning into vibrations that align with your desires.

But in order to do that, you must become deeply and continuously aware of your energy, thoughts, and feelings – and the seven different ways in which they shape your reality.

How to maintain law of attraction

The law of attraction suggests that you can attract positive or negative things into your life through your thoughts and actions. It relies on the theory that everything is made up of energy, so the type of energy you put out will come back to you. If you're ready to use the law of attraction to tell the universe what you want, start by creating a positive mindset so that you can send out positive energy. Then, take action toward your goals and confront your setbacks with a good attitude.

METHOD 1 : Creating a Positive Mindset

1. **Visualize your dreams coming true.**

Close your eyes and picture yourself living the life you want. Imagine doing your dream job, showing off your talents, or sliding into your new car. Do this every day to solidify your intentions and bring them one step closer to reality.

- Always picture yourself being successful. For example, imagine yourself getting a promotion at work, not just going about your day-to-day activities. You don't want to just get the job; you want to excel at it.

2. **Focus on what you want in your life, not what you're lacking.**

Don't think about your old, broken down car. Instead, picture yourself driving a new car. This puts the focus on what you want to bring into your life, rather than what you want to eliminate. It sends the message to the universe that you expect good things to happen!

- The idea behind this is that what you're thinking about is what you want in your life. So if you think, "I wish I had a car that didn't break down all the time," you're still focusing on your old car, not a new one.

- As another example, think to yourself, "I'm studying hard to get a good grade," rather than, "I hope I don't fail this semester."

3. **Phrase your desires using positive terms.** It's important to avoid phrases that rely on negative words like "no" or "not" to state what you want, such as "I don't want to lose my job." Similarly, include the words for what you want to avoid attracting the wrong thing. For instance, "I don't want to lose" sends out the word "lose," while "I want to win" sends out the word "win."

4. **Express gratitude for what you already have.** Appreciating the good things in your life helps you feel better about your life, which supports your positive mindset. List the things you're grateful for aloud, or write them in a gratitude journal. Additionally, thank people for the good things they add to your life.

   - For example, write 3 things you're grateful for every morning before you get out of bed. This helps you start your day in a good mood

5. **Meditate at least 5 minutes a day to lower your stress levels.** Stress is a normal part of life, but too much can be overwhelming. Relieve your daily stresses with a short meditation that will relax both your mind and body. For a simple meditation, sit in a comfortable position, then close your eyes. Focus on your breathing, letting your thoughts come and go.

   - You can find guided meditations online or through an app like Calm, Headspace, or Insight Timer.

   - Meditation can also help you become more aware of your emotional state, which in turn will help you regulate your emotions more effectively.

   - Meditating effectively takes practice. Make it a goal to meditate on a daily basis.

6. **Replace your worries with thoughts about how things could go right.** Worrying can make you manifest what you're trying to avoid. When worries happen, challenge them by questioning how likely they are to happen. Then, think about what has happened in the past when you worried. Next, consider how bad the worst-case scenario would be if your worried thoughts actually happened. You'll likely realize it's not that big of a deal in the long-run.

   - For example, let's say you're worried you'll embarrass yourself during a presentation. How likely is that to happen? Has it happened before? If you did mess up, would it really matter? Would you still think about it a year later? You'll likely recognize your worry isn't really a big deal.

- It also helps to think about what your life might be like in 5 or 10 years. Will the thing you're worried about even matter then? Probably not. For example, you might worry about failing a test, but you likely won't even remember the test in 5 years.

7. **Give yourself time to learn how to stay positive because it can be hard.** At first, it will be hard for you to keep your thoughts positive. It's natural for negative thoughts to come back to you. However, you can help yourself focus on the positive by intentionally confronting negative thoughts. Acknowledge them, dismiss them, then replace them with something positive. With practice, you can become more positive over time.

   - For example, you might catch yourself thinking, "I keep working so hard, but I don't seem to be getting anywhere." Stop yourself for a moment and think about why you're having this thought. Then, list the positive things you've experienced while working on this goal, such as learning new things or having new experiences. Finally, choose to see something positive in the situation. You might tell yourself, "I'm getting better over time, and I'm proud of my progress."

   - After a while, the positive thoughts that you're choosing to have on a conscious level will become part of your subconscious mind, and positive thinking will become more automatic for you.

7 Simple Steps: How to Use the Law of Attraction in Life

In 2006, a book was published and since then it has become a worldwide publishing phenomenon, translating into more than 50 languages, sold more than 20 million copies and has grossed over $300 million in sales by 2009.

The book is none other than the groundbreaking "The Secret". The Secret is a huge success and the content is based on one a powerful principle that everyone wants to learn, the Law of Attraction. The Secret popularizes the Law of Attraction and today, many people talk about it and want to know how to make it work.

And this is exactly what you are going to discover in this article. You will discover the 7 simple steps that you can use to activate the Law of Attraction in your life to achieve whatever you want.

The fundamental principle behind the Law of Attraction is that you will become what you think about most of the time. And thus, you can achieve your goals and materialize your dreams if you choose to consciously think about them on a regular basis.

Of course, this is only the fundamental. There is more than this if you want to make the law works in your life. Like the Aladdin lamp, once you have it with you, you can make your wishes come true, but you must know how to summon the genie to come forth.

The problem with most people is that they have no idea how to summon the genie. They have heard about the Aladdin lamp that can grant them any wish, but they have no idea how to use the magical lamp.

The same goes for the Law of Attraction. Most people understand what it is, but many did not know the real secret behind to make it work.

Below are the 7 simple steps that you must follow in order to activate the Law of Attraction and manifest whatever you desire in your life.

1. Decide

The first step you need to do to use the Law of Attraction is to decide on what you want. You have to be crystal clear with your vision and the things that you want to be, do and have in your life.

Most people never go through this step and they wonder why the law did not work on them. It is just like goal setting, you must be crystal clear with what you want. Don't just say that you want to be rich or be happy.

These are vague requests and often, vague goals will produce vague results. Don't just say that you want to travel the world. You will end up going places that you don't want to. Therefore, be crystal clear with what you want.

Imagine you get into a cab and the driver asks you where you would like to go. What is your answer? If you say, "anywhere will do", guess what, the driver will chase you out or simply bring you anywhere. The same goes in life. If you have no idea what you want, life will throw anything at you.

And the same goes for the Law of Attraction. You must be clear with your request. Your desire is not clear, you will manifest whatever that comes to you. The Universe will be confused with your request and thus, fail to give you the result you want.

Start by asking yourself questions such as what do you want to be, what experiences do you want to have, where do you want to live and with who?

Your first step of deciding exactly what you want will become the fundamental of your manifestation. If your fundamental is blurry, you will not go far and your goals will never be realized.

Action Step:

Be absolutely clear with what you want. The more detail it is, the better. The message you send to the Universe will be clear and so it will be easier for you to manifest.

2. Ask

The second step you need to take is to ask for it. Once you have decided on what you want, you must then write it down and ask for it.

For instance, you can write down the car that you want to own on paper in present tense.

Here is an example:

I am so happy and satisfy now that I own a black BMW i5 and I'm driving it to work each day.

Don't ask in the future tense such as "I'm going to own a BMW i5". You must ask in the present tense as if you are living your goals.

Plus, use the word "I", because this word refers to yourself and it gives you a strong sense of ownership.

Besides that, remember to include emotional words such as "happy", "joyful", "satisfy", "thrill", "grateful", "enjoy", etc. These words are powerful because they bring out your emotions and make your asking process stronger and more realistic.

More importantly, you must be willing to ask for it daily. Make sure you refer to what you want every single day. It is just like practicing daily goal setting. Choose to write it down, review it, and think about it every single day.

The key is that you want to consciously turn what you want into your subconscious mind. You want to consciously program your goals, your dreams, and your wishes into your subconscious mind so that you can tap into the power of the Universe to manifest them.

Action Step:

Write down what you want and ask for them each day. You must consciously think about the things that you want to be, do, and have regularly so that you can program them into your subconscious.

3. Visualize

One of the most powerful steps that most people miss out while using the Law of Attraction is that they did not visualize what they want. And this is what you need to do in this step.

Do you know that visualization is a powerful technique that has been proven by science on its effectiveness in achieving what you want or improving your skills?

In fact, many professional athletes use visualization to train and improve their skills to a higher level. This is simply because our brain cannot differentiate between what is real and what is imagined.

Thus, when you visualize, your brain will create new neural pathways and close the gap between what is happening in your physical world with your imagination.

John Assaraf, the famous guru who has been featured in The Secret is known for his story of manifesting his house through vision boards.

A vision board is a collection of the pictures of what you want and it is used to help you visualize the achievement of your goals. Some people find it difficult to visualize the things that they want, and hence, a vision board can be helpful in this.

Furthermore, you don't just visualize the things that you want for once only and hope that the Universe will manifest them into your life. You have practice visualization and do it on a regular basis.

It may be true that sometimes it is difficult to imagine the things that you are yet to own, especially in the beginning, and this is why you need to practice it often, preferably, on a daily basis.

Experts have shown that the best time to practice visualization is once in the morning after you wake up and once at night before you go to sleep.

Always remember this quote, "repetition is the mother of all skills". So don't just visualize once and then forget it. Do it on a daily basis. You can become good at visualization if you practice it enough.

And when you are good at visualizing the things that you want, the chances that the Law of Attraction will work for you will greatly increase.

Action Step:

Commit to visualization. Schedule a time each day to practice visualization. Choose a quiet place, sit down comfortably, close your eyes and imagine that you have already achieved all the goals you desire. Create a vision board to help you in this.

4. Feel It

Do you know why most people say that visualization and affirmation did not work? The main reason is that they did not include emotions into their practice when they visualize or affirm their goals.

You have to understand that emotion plays an important part in manifesting what you want and in the activation of the Law of Attraction.

If you are just visualizing the goals you want for the sake of doing the visualization, it will never work out for you. Don't just do it for the sake of doing it, you must include emotions and feelings into it.

Imagine that you are in a lecture hall listening to your lecturer giving his talk but he is not passionate at all. Do you think you will be interested to sit in the lecture hall for the passionless talk or do you think you will be able to absorb a lot from the lecturer? No, you will not.

Now imagine you are visiting a car showroom and all the salesman did is to read you all the information of the car from a brochure. Do you think you will be interested to buy the car? Not at all, even if you did buy the car, it is not because of the salesman, right?

The same works for the Law of Attraction. The Universe is listening to what you are saying all the time. Hence, if you are not persuasive, if you are not passionate, and if you are not putting in any feelings and emotions into what you desire, do you think the Universe will manifest them for you? You know the answer.

At a deeper level, thoughts are vibrations. And with emotions and feelings, you can send your thoughts to the Universe through a stronger and more powerful channel.

When you are visualizing what you want, make sure you add as many details as possible. See it as though it is real and is happening right now. Add in your five senses and feel the emotions.

Try to imagine vividly that you walk to your fridge, open the door, and you see a large yellow lemon in there. You reach out to the lemon and take it with your hand. Feel the texture. Now, imagine vivid that you take the lemon to your kitchen, and you use a knife and cut it into halves. See the juices oozing and now, take one piece of the lemon, squeeze the juice into your mouth. How do you feel?

Do you feel you have more saliva in your mouth right now? Well, if you imagine it vividly with all the details and you include your senses, your mouth will produce more saliva.

The reason being that your mind will think that your imagination is real and react to it. This is why you must include feelings and emotions into your visualization and affirmations.

Action Steps:

Every time when you practice visualization or affirmation, make sure you include your emotions and feelings into it. See the picture as real as possible and feel it with your senses. The more emotion you associate with your visualization, the more powerful and effective it will be.

5. Gratitude

Another important key step most people miss out is gratitude. The majority of people are so busy in visualizing their dreams and making lists for their goals that they forget about gratitude, which is a crucial key to making the Law of Attraction to work.

Gratitude is important in manifesting what you want in life because it raises your vibration and brings you into harmony with the Universe. In fact, gratitude is so powerful that it can change and transform your life.

To make it simple to understand, when you are grateful for everything that is happening to you, you will live better, you will feel that you have enough, you will feel loved, happy and fulfilled. In other words, you are operating from a life of abundance.

On the other hand, if you are not grateful for everything that is happening to you, you will complain, you feel that everything is wrong, you struggle to pay your bills, you feel that your spouse cheats on you, and everything is not going right. You are operating from a life of lack.

Gratitude creates a life of abundance while complaining creates a life of scarcity.

Can you see now why the attitude of gratitude is important in your life right now? And because your thinking will create the vibration energy, so if you are thinking negatively, complaining and blaming all the time, your thought energy will not be in coherence with the Universe.

Meanwhile, when you are grateful, when you are feeling happy, and you appreciate all that you have right now, you are transmitting a positive energy to the Universe.

Anthony Robbins once asked John Templeton what is the secret to wealth. Guess what Sir Templeton answered? He answered Tony, "You know it. You teach it, it's gratitude".

And here is the explanation from Sir Templeton, the investment pioneer who turned $10,000 into billions during the World War 2 era:

"Because if you have a billion dollars, and every day you live pissed off and frustrated, the quality of your life is called pissed off and frustrated. But if you have next to nothing, and are grateful for whatever it is you have, you're the richest person that you're going to know. It doesn't matter how much money you've got if you don't have gratitude."

So make sure you are grateful for everything that you already manifested and what you are about to receive.

When you are grateful for the things that you want, it shows that you confirm to the Universe that they are already yours and that you are open to receiving them.

Action Steps:

Here is what you can do to live your life with gratitude. Every day, practice writing a gratitude list. Write down everything that you are grateful for. It can be your car, your dog, your cat, your children, your wife, your job, your boss, your house, your computer, etc, anything you can think of and be grateful for.

Use the word, "thank you" more often and express your appreciation to everything that is happening in your life. More importantly, feel the emotion of thankfulness and gratefulness.

Take Action on Your Dreams

One of the core reasons people fail to achieve what they want through the Law of Attraction is that they don't do anything besides thinking about it.

If you only choose to think about what you want, you will never manifest what you want. Law of Attraction is more than just thinking. Money will not fall from the sky and your dreams will not come true without action.

Action is the link bridge between your dreams and your reality. If you want to bring forth what you want from your dreams, you must connect your reality with your dreams, through action.

Therefore, take massive and consistent action to accomplish your goals and achieve your dreams. Do something, work on what you want and always be on the move.

6. Trust and Believe

This step is where the magic happens. In order to activate the Law of Attraction and to make it work, you must trust and believe wholeheartedly for what you have asked for. Sincerely trust and believe that it will happen.

Most people fail with the attraction process because they don't believe that they can manifest what they want. They imagine that they become a millionaire and earn a huge amount of money, but deep down, they don't believe that it is going to happen to them.

When you do not believe that things are possible, you are sabotaging yourself in your mind. Your thoughts and not in alignment with your action. What you think and what you do will not be in coherence.

Take buying the lottery as an example. If you do not believe that you stand a chance to win, you will never buy the lottery ticket. You don't even bother about it. However, if you truly believe that there is a chance that you can win, you will go ahead and buy a lottery ticket.

Your committed action will show whether you believe it or not. If you believe that you cannot fail, you will do whatever it takes because you know that whatever you do, you will succeed. Conversely, if you do not believe that you can succeed and you believe that you will fail, you will never take action or try it.

This is why a lot of people fail to take action because they don't believe that things are possible in the first place.

They say that they want to be a millionaire and build a successful business, but you will never see they put in the effort and take action to make their dreams a reality. They simply do not believe that it is possible for them.

Successful people attract their dreams and achieve their goals because they are always in action. They believe that things are possible and that is why they take action.

To make it simple, you will never do it if you don't believe in it. Therefore, to use the Law of Attraction, you must believe that whatever you ask for is possible.

Action Steps:

Always do a self-reflection on what you do in life. Are you taking action or are you not? If you are not taking action, it shows that you don't believe that you can achieve what you desire in life.

Remember this quote, "You are what you do, not what you say you will do". Most people say and talk about their goals, but they don't include actions because, at the bottom of their heart, they don't believe they can achieve what they want.

7. Receive

The final step you need to take is to receive. After going through all the steps, you must be ready to receive for what you have asked for.

And sometimes in order to receive, you must let go. You can never start a new relationship if you still hold on to the old. If you want to buy a new car, sell off your old car. If you want to buy new clothes, get rid of your old clothes and make space for the new.

You can only start a new life when you clear off the old and make way for the new. Most people still hold on to their old beliefs, habits, mindset, and behaviors, and they wonder why the Universe is not bringing them what they want.

Imagine that you are a sponge and everything that is around you and happening to you is water. If a sponge is full, it cannot take in more water. If you are full, you cannot take in new things.

What you need to do then is to squeeze the sponge to let go release the water. And when you are empty again, you then allow yourself to take in and receive new things from your life.

Here is a very meaningful saying to illustrate the principle of letting go and be ready to receive:

"You cannot discover new oceans unless you have the courage to lose sight of the shore."

Therefore, be prepared and get ready to let go to receive what the Universe has in store for you.

Action Steps:

There are many ways how you can practice this final step of receiving. One of them is through giving. Learn to give so that you can receive in your life.

If you want to thrive in your business, learn to create more value to your clients. If you want other people to treat you with care, be the first to care for others. If you want to be successful, solve other people's problems.

You can start from a simple act of kindness. Smile and greet strangers, hold the door for someone, buy food for the needy, and create more value to receive more in life.

How to Apply the Law of Attraction: 3 Proven Techniques

What we tell ourselves matters. If your internal dialogue is an unbroken string of insults about your body, your work performance, and your past then guess what? Achieving your dreams will be next to impossible.

You don't have to be a star athlete to realize that Olympic champions don't earn gold medals by exercising once a week and eating buckets of fried chicken. No, they achieve their goals by training their bodies.

Well, in order to succeed you have to train your mind just as fiercely. If you train your mind to believe the absolute worst things about yourself, then the worst is exactly what you will get.

The sad truth is few of us would ever speak to a stranger let alone a close friend the way we often speak to ourselves. We really are our own worst enemy. That's unfortunate.

Why? Because how we speak to ourselves has a lot to do with our actions. If you want to achieve your dreams, it's important to learn how to apply the law of attraction. Here's some tips.

Attraction Explained

Although often misattributed to Gautama Buddha, regardless of its source I think this quote explains the law of attraction perfectly.

"What you think you become. What you feel you attract. What you imagine you create." In other words, start manifesting! After studying with Buddhist monks, psychologist and researcher Richard Davidson discovered how even short-term meditation can bring about changes in gene expression. This is how genes encode proteins, which then determines the function of a cell.

So by manifesting a positive outlook for ourselves and our career we can not only alter our perspective but set ourselves upon the path toward achieving it. As Davidson points out, people can be trained to develop awareness, connection, insight, and purpose.

The law of attraction is premised on the idea that like attracts like. If you manifest a positive outlook, you'll get positive results. If you view your future negatively, you'll get negative results.

It doesn't matter whether or not you believe in the law of attraction. If you decide not to believe in gravity, it won't make the ground any softer when you fall out of a tree. Understanding how to apply the law of attraction isn't a free ticket to riches.

Believing the universe will make you wealthy isn't the same as telling yourself that you deserve success, you will work your butt off to succeed at your goals, and the universe will help you during your journey.

As the old cliche goes, the harder you work, the luckier you will get. Still, working 80-hour weeks while encased in an impenetrable prison of negativity isn't a recipe for success.

Instead, change your internal dialogue. Retrain yourself to celebrate what you have already accomplished. Instead of criticizing your thighs, congratulate yourself for going on a jog. Don't obsess over an embarrassment from last year, focus on an achievement from last week.

Practice Gratitude

It's so easy to obsess over the things we don't have. The problem is, no one ever has everything. Even if you buy a bigger house or a newer car, it's no guarantee you'll be satisfied. You'll likely still want more. Yet the truth is, for most people, life is pretty amazing.

A few centuries ago even the wealthiest kings lived in drafty, rat-infested castles facing death from myriad diseases or their own people. Today you likely had enough to eat and a roof over your head. Yet even those who lack those things find room for gratitude. So start your day making a list of the things you are grateful for.

It can be simple like a great cup of coffee or a good night's sleep. It could be a recent promotion or a new relationship. Writing down what you are grateful for will help train your mind.

Plus, in one study, participants who kept a gratitude journal for two weeks had fewer headaches, less stomach pain, clearer skin, and reduced congestion. In other words just writing down the things they were grateful for gave them more reasons to be grateful!

After you've made a gratitude list, try meditating for a few minutes. Learning to be present is another secret on how to apply the law of attraction.

That's because much of our negative self talk is based on the past; most of our stressful anxiety is concerned with the future. The present is the one thing we can immediately affect by focusing on the good things we have each day. The law of attraction is not a pollyanna ritual nor a command to always be happy.

Life is about balance, there will be bad along with good. No, the key is identifying those good things and appreciating them in the moment.

Visualize

Going back to the Olympic athlete, they of course do more than just train their body. They train their mind as well. Anytime there's a conversation about visualization, a sports star is often named. That's because there's a clear line between visualizing victory and the result. Regular life is more complex than a tournament. Yet just as an athlete pictures not just the trophy and the championship, you need to see not just the promotion or successful business but the steps you will take to get there. The best time to visualize is when you are at your most relaxed -- often in the morning or the evening. Close your eyes. Then imagine the steps you will take to achieve success.

After creating a vivid picture, you can work a SMART program -- for Specific, Measurable, Attainable, Relevant and Time-bound goals. Ask yourself what it is that you truly desire. Be honest. Retraining our internal monologue and manifesting positive energy isn't easy. Still, I firmly believe the time you devote to it will be time well spent.

The Ultimate Guide to the Law of Attraction — For Beginners

Knowing how to use the Law of Attraction can be super beneficial on the road to happiness and success. Here's how you can manifest your dream life.

Ever since Rhonda Byrne wrote The Secret in 2006, the Law of Attraction has become one of the most controversial topics in modern society.

But now, there have been several studies done on the effectiveness of the Law of Attraction.

In fact, one interesting study about prayer and pregnancy showed the ability we, as humans, have to influence matters and fulfill our desires, particularly through prayer, which is known to be a powerful tool for manifestation. The results showed women who had been prayed for showed almost twice the rate of pregnancy as those who hadn't been prayed for.

Is the Law of Attraction Real?

The Law of Attraction isn't some perplexing hocus pocus, like Mary Poppins' magical carry-all carpet bag. It's continuously at work with or without your intention. And when you are aware of the Law of Attraction and understand how to use it in your life, it attracts the things you desire to your life. So, yes, it is very real.

There are many everyday examples of the Law of Attraction at work:

- When you're looking to buy a new car (or just bought one), then you start seeing that car everywhere.

- Thinking about someone and they show up at your doorstep.

- Or even craving sushi and your partner suggests it for dinner.

And now, explore how to hold that good-feeling belief so that the Law of Attraction will work for you.

Things to keep in mind

Before getting down on how to apply the Law of Attraction to your life, it's important to keep a few things in mind.

12 laws of the Universe

The 12 intrinsic, unchanging laws of our universe work in synergy as guiding principles. No single law can defy another.

Here's an example: the Law of Resonance works hand in hand with the Law of Attraction. It states that when the vibration of a thing is projected, it will attract energies of the same resonance.

However, if the energy vibrations aren't on the same frequency, then one will prevail over the other.

Meaning, if you're working on manifesting abundance, but on a subconscious level, you're wired around scarcity and fears, then you will keep attracting scarcity and fears.

So, because the laws of the universe work as a collective for the betterment of your life, don't expect to be able to manifest floating away on a magical parrot-headed umbrella whenever there's a shift in the wind. (Check out lucid dreaming if you want to do that.) None of us are Mary Poppins, after all, no matter how many spoonfuls of sugar we take.

Free will

Everything in this universe has free will. In other words, your desires and manifestations must follow this principle. You can master the Law of Attraction and attract whatever you wish for, but if it violates somebody's free will, it will not serve you well.

Your intentions vs other people's intentions

You're also competing with other people's intentions – both good and bad. So, be aware that if your desire is in direct conflict with someone else's stronger desire, the universe will respond accordingly.

The Law of Attraction does not give you full and total control of your life, it simply states that like will attract like. And you can use this to your advantage by being intentional with your desires, but this isn't magic.

The reality is, your thoughts and feelings have an effect on the events that take place around you. When you practice the Law of Attract, shift your perspective, and understand the truth about your relationship to the universe, only then can you begin to attract better things into your life.

How to Use the Law of Attraction

The formula for how to use the Law of Attraction is simple:

- Decide what you really want.
- Raise your frequency to match your desire.
- Open up to the possibilities and believe in them fully.
- Pretend you already have what you want–and enjoy the feeling!
- Persistence is key.

Now keep in mind that the Law of Attraction and manifestation work hand in hand. The Law of Attraction is the universal principle of 'like attracting like,' while manifestation is when you consciously use your thoughts and energy to attract your sincerest desires.

So, start thinking about what you want to manifest into your life — such as money, love, relationships, health, and spirituality — to make the power of the Law of Attraction work for you.

Now, let's take a closer look at how the Law of Attraction steps can be used to your advantage.

Step 1: Make your decision

You need a 20/20 vision of your desire. Whether you wish to attract something minor or you're looking for a huge overhaul of your life, be clear about what you truly want.

Imagine what this new thing looks like, smells like, sounds like, feels like, and tastes like (if it's relevant).

- How do you feel once this new thing is in your life?
- Where do you feel it in your body?
- Does it make your toes tingle or make your heart flutter?
- Does your pulse race or do you feel a wave of calm?

Make it real in your mind. Don't just focus on receiving this new thing, but think about your life after you receive it too. Imagine how it will change your world.

Taking part in this imagination exercise, you align yourself with your desires. Open up to the possibilities and prepare your body to receive whatever it is you are attempting to attract. It may seem simple, but this first step is what paves the way to working with the energies of the Law of Attraction.

Step 2: Practice unconditional love

Being aware of your thoughts and feelings is incredibly important. When you love yourself, you open up the possibility to receive your greatest desires, and you begin to only desire the things that are best for you.

But if you feel as though you don't deserve what you're seeking, those deep, subconscious fears and doubts send messages that compete with your desire. The only effective method for combating fears and doubts is to become aware of them, acknowledge them, and approach them with love and compassion.

Step 3: Open up to the possibilities

First, think about the bad things in your life right now. Can you see connections to your fears, doubts, and old patterns that led those things into your life?

Focus on understanding your part in this overall process, rather than feeling guilty or ashamed. Recognizing how your fears have manifested in your life doesn't mean that the bad things in your life are your fault. It simply means that the Law of Attraction has responded to the signal you sent out.

Next, think of all the great things in your life. Reflect upon how your hopes, dreams, and ambition attracted those good things to you. Reinforce in your mind how, when you believe something can happen, it does.

Again, rather than experiencing pride or feeling boastful, this is about understanding and seeing how the Law of Attraction is already a part of your life. It's always existed, but now you are aware of it.

Once you see that the Law of Attraction works without you knowing, it will reinforce your understanding that this is simply a universal law. Work with your awareness of the law and understand how it works. Then you can work with the law and align yourself with it.

Step 4: Experience the reality of your desires

Now, it's time to live the reality of your desires.

This is a bit of an acting exercise, so let go of your inhibitions to make this exercise really effective. Rather than just visualizing the reality in your mind, live it as much as possible.

If you're using the system to find, let's say, great parking, get in your car and drive to that parking spot with the full intention and expectation of finding it clear for you. Announce it out loud. "That parking spot is clear for me. I am parking in a spot that is open for me."

If you're trying to lose weight, go out and buy an outfit that fits the size you're aiming for. If you want a new car, go to a dealership and shop around. Or, if you're aiming for something as big as complete financial freedom, start planning what you're going to do with all that free time and money.

The important step is to take action and act as if you already have what you're looking for. Jump into this step with joy and enthusiasm. When you take action as if you've already gotten what you desire, you are sending a huge, loud, and clear message to the universe that you're serious. Actions speak louder than words, right?

Step 5: Be patient, yet persistent

There's no formula for how long things take to manifest in your life. Some people begin to see things happen immediately, while others take a little more time. But the key here is patience and persistence.

Continue to express gratitude and appreciation every day. Think positively and recall all the connections you made that prove the Law of Attraction is real for you. Take time every day to review the visualization exercises and prep your mind and body to receive this incredible gift.

How to Apply the Law of Attraction

While manifesting, you may come across challenges. Here are some exercises you can do while you're working with the Law of Attraction.

- Make a vision board
- Do a visualization meditation
- Write a gratitude list
- Practice mindfulness

- Practice kindness
- Be focused and intentional
- Repeat empowering affirmations
- Express yourself through movement

Practice any or all of the Law of Attraction exercises you want to, but we suggest trying each exercise at least once. There are no hard and fast rules, so feel free to tweak these exercises and make them your own.

In addition, try these 12 hacks to manifest more abundance in your life.

How Can the Law of Attraction Improve Your Life?

Now that we've covered what the Law of Attraction is and how it works, let's get into the ways you can use it to improve your life.

1. Attract money

Financial abundance is the number one reason people become interested in the Law of Attraction. It's no wonder. Working tirelessly for small paychecks is exhausting and when life starts throwing unexpected expenses your way, debt can seem inevitable.

The good news is that the Law of Attraction money is easy to come by. Once you learn the techniques, you'll start to see changes really quickly. Many people report unexpected checks and seemingly random job opportunities. Even literally finding money is some of the first results when working with the Law of Attraction.

2. Manifest love and relationships

The second most popular reason people seek information about the Law of Attraction is to find true love. Finding a lifetime partner to fulfill an ideal, loving relationship can seem like an elusive and frustrating game that you can't win.

Luckily, the Law of Attraction is a great tool for finding love. Because the Law of Attraction means working on yourself and your desires, it inherently makes you a more attractive person with a clear vision of what you want and needs in your life.

3. Improve your health

Most people don't consider using the Law of Attraction to bring better health into their lives. However, as you noticed in the results of the aging experiment, it's actually a great tool for that purpose. Because the Law of Attraction works with thoughts and thoughts affect our physical reality, you may be attracting poor health into your life right now without even realizing it.

Learning about the Law of Attraction helps you see that your thoughts are having a direct effect on your entire world. That includes the vessel you're traveling in. A good attitude goes a long way to improving your health. The Law of Attraction can help you take that even further.

4. Spiritual awakening

By its very nature, the Law of Attraction connects you with higher, spiritual planes of existence. When you start practicing the techniques, you begin to see beyond the mundane, ordinary world. A new, brighter world opens up to you that is brimming with possibility.

Many people find a spiritual awakening in those possibilities. Connecting with the rhythms of the universe and opening up to new potentials awakens the spiritual force inside you that is connected to everything around you. The Law of Attraction demonstrates that you are connected to everything and everything is connected to you.

5. Have more fun

The results of using the Law of Attraction techniques are only limited by your imagination. By the laws of physics, you're not going to manifest bird-like flying anytime soon.

There are endless things you can attract in your life. From practical things — like 'good parking karma' that can guarantee you a great parking spot, to 'calls to adventure' that open you up to random invitations to explore the world — you can use the principles behind the Law of Attraction in any way you please.

Law of Attraction Books to Inspire You

If you're not ready to dive in headfirst and just want to dip your toes in, books are a great way to start. Here are a few recommended ones:

- The Secret by Rhona Byrne
- The Universe Has Your Back by Gabby Bernstein
- Think and Grow Rich by Napolean Hill
- The Power of Now by Eckhart Tolle
- The Power of Intention by Dr. Wayne Dyer
- Infinite Possibilities: The Art of Living Your Dreams by Mike Dooley
- Manifest: 7 Steps to Living Your Best Life by Roxie Nafousi

Regardless of what you're looking to attract, using the Law of Attraction can get confusing for some people. But with a sprinkle of inspiration from these books, you may just find that using the Law of Attraction can be a powerful tool.

Ways The 'Law Of Attraction' Can Improve Your Life

Psychologists, New Age thinkers and religious leaders have been talking about the Law Of Attraction for years, though it gained popularity again when the book "The Secret" made waves in 2006.

The law is simply this: We attract whatever we think about, good or bad.

Oprah is a fan of the law and devoted an episode of her show to how it could change lives.

Whether or not you believe in the power of the universe, there is scientific research that proves the effects of positive thinking.

We've highlighted the most compelling elements from one of the most popular books on the topic, The Law of Attraction: The Basics of the Teachings of Abraham, by Esther and Jerry Hicks.

You attract good or bad experiences based on your thoughts.

"The one who speaks most about illness has illness. The one who speaks about prosperity has prosperity," Esther and Jerry Hicks write. "You attract all of it." By focusing on something, you make it happen.

Thinking about something means you invite it in, even if you don't want it.

"When you think a little thought of something that you want, through the Law of Attraction, that thought grows larger and larger, and more and more powerful," according to the book. So keep your thoughts positive.

The more you focus on something, the more powerful it becomes.

This allows you to create your own reality by "attracting" the experiences you want to have. You probably brought bad things upon yourself by worrying about them, according to the laws described in the book.

It's better to trust your emotions than over-think a decision.

In other words: Listen to your intuition. Instead of overthinking your choices, let your emotions guide you toward what is right and what is wrong. This will result in a more satisfying life.

You can make good things happen more quickly by thinking about them more..

"Want" and "desire" consist of wanting "to focus attention, or give thought toward a subject, while at the same time experiencing positive emotion. When you give your attention to a subject and you feel only positive emotion about it as you do so, it will come very quickly into your experience," the Hicks write.

To make a change, you've got to see things as you hope them to be, not as they are.

This is something that successful people know about. It's also called visualization. Michael Phelps spoke about picturing himself winning every night before bed.

"In order to effect true positive change in your experience, you must disregard how things are — as well as how others are seeing you — and give more of your attention to the way you prefer things to be," the book says.

You can increase your magnetic power by devoting time to "powerful thinking." each day.

Spend 15 minutes every day thinking hard about your goals, dreams and what you want from life. The Hicks say this increases your chances for success.

Success isn't a finite resource; everyone can have it.

Others being successful doesn't limit your success. And by attracting abundance to yourself, you are not limiting another, according to the book.

Don't allow yourself to wallow in disappointment.

Being disappointed only attracts more stuff to be upset about and is only a sign that you're not getting what you want in life. So think about how to get what you want instead of what you don't have.

Avoid TV shows that deal with negative experiences like crime or illness.

Letting this stuff in makes you think about it more and increases the odds it could happen to you. "Your attention to anything is drawing it closer to you," they say.

Know that your relationships with people are bad because you made them that way.

Giving your attention to the negative can wreak havoc on personal relationships. This mentality can help free us from bad relationships with relatives or a spouse. "Nothing can come into your experience without your personal attraction to it," they say.

Don't worry about what you're dreaming; instead use your dreams as a guide.

Dreams might provide some insight into the psyche, but you're not in the process of "creating" while you're asleep, the book says.

How to Use the Law of Attraction for Specific Goals

Now let's take a look at some examples of how to use the law of attraction to manifest specific outcomes in your life.

Attract Money & Financial Success

If you would like to grow your wealth, spend more time thinking about money!

Read books and watch videos on how to increase your prosperity and make more money. Envision the exact amount you would like and by when. Simply believe it will happen, and it very much will.

Above all, remember to be thankful for everything that you already have and appreciate the abundance of all that's good in your life. This will help you create a vibrational match for the financial abundance that you want in your future.

Love & Relationship Attraction

People who are able to harness the power of the Law of Attraction frequently use it to attract more love and romance into their lives. If you want to attract love into your life, be the love you want to attract!

Be loving and generous with others and yourself. Appreciate the love you do have in your life and look for ways to express it. The more you create a vibration of love, the stronger the signal you will send to the Universe and gain more power to attract love into your life.

Improve Your Well-Being

You can also use this universal law to improve your mental and physical health.

Learning how to use the law of attraction effectively requires you to become a more positive person who focuses on feeling soul-enriching emotions such as gratitude, connection, and abundance.

This allows you to cultivate a healthier mindset, which in turn will inspire you to feel more confident and be inspired to take better care of your physical health as well.

Manifest Success Into Your Life

If you're wondering whether it really is possible to use this universal law to take control of your destiny and attract more success into your life, I'm living proof!

And I owe it all to my mentor, W. Clement Stone. When I was a teacher in Chicago making $8,000 a year, he told me, "I want you to set a goal that's so big that if you achieve it, you'll know it's because of the secret I am teaching you."

I decided my goal would be to make $100,000 that year. I created an image of a $100,000 dollar bill and hung it on the ceiling above my bed. Every morning I'd see the image. I'd visualize what it would be like to have $100,000. Everything I did was to achieve that goal. At the end of the year, I had made $97,000!

But that's just one story... watch the video below to see other incredible stories of people who have used this universal law to achieve incredible success in their lives.

Law of Attraction Meditation for Guidance

Meditation is an excellent form of practice to activate the law of attraction and cultivate a clear, positive mind.

Here, try this simple meditation practice to energize awareness:

- Find a quiet place, close your eyes, and focus on slowing down your breathing.
- Repeat an uplifting word or phrase.
- Move into a state of quiet.
- Imagine yourself surrounded by a sphere of light.

If you are new to the practice of meditation, your thoughts will drift and your mind will wander at first. Remember not to be hard on yourself when this happens. This is just part of learning how to meditate.

The point isn't to control your thoughts or try to empty your head of thoughts (both of which are impossible). It's simply to become more aware of your thoughts. Once you notice yourself thinking thoughts that are negative or don't serve you, let them go and bring your mind back to the present.

Consistent practice of meditation will help clear your mind of distractions, cleanse your thoughts, and enhance your spiritual connection with the Universe. This will naturally help you be a more positive person and attract more good into your life.

Law of Attraction Quotes

Throughout history, the greatest minds and spiritual teachers have understood the power our thoughts have over our lives. Here are 10 Law of Attraction quotes to inspire you to activate its potential in your own life.

Take Action Today

Now that you understand the power of the Law of Attraction and how it works, I encourage you to start putting it to work in your life right away!

Remember these tips:

Are you ready to put the power of the universe to work in your life?

- **Your thoughts determine your reality:** If you want to change your life, you must start by changing your thoughts. When you cultivate an "attitude of gratitude" and train yourself to focus on what's good in life, you will find your life filled with more positive people and experiences!

- **Dream big:** If you want the Universe to deliver big results, you must have big dreams! Remember, the Universe always responds to the energy you send out.

- **Use positive affirmations:** The best way to keep your thoughts, actions, and energy focused on your highest goals is to use positive affirmations. When you affirm your goals as already being achieved, you activate your subconscious mind to make your vision a reality!

- **Clarify your goals:** A clear vision leads to clear results. That's why it's so important to be direct on what you want – and to confirm that what you think you want really is what you want. Ambiguous desires get ambiguous results.

- **Use a vision board:** Vision boards are a powerful tool for clarifying your vision for your life and keeping your goals top of mind so you can effortlessly attract them into your life.

If so, be sure to grab my free guide on how to Activate the Law of Attraction and harness the power of effortless success.

This helpful guide will give you detailed information on how to manifest what you want in every area of your life by mastering your thoughts and emotions so you can attract the life you truly want—as well as experience more joy, peace, and abundance in everything you do!

How to Start Using the Law of Attraction in Your Life

It doesn't matter at what stage you are at on your manifesting journey, there is always more to learn about the Law of Attraction. Manifesting doesn't go on vacation, which is why when you start using the Law of Attraction and consistently keep using it to its full potential, this is when you begin to understand that manifestations occur in very subtle ways every minute of the day.

Becoming more mindful of your own thoughts helps you to discover what you should keep or remove from your own mind and the reality of your experience.

You will become more attentive to underlying negativity and can start to combat it with new beliefs and feelings that better reflect your positive vision of the coming days.

This ongoing focus on self-reflection also enables you to start seeing what you really want from your future, and you can then progress to formulating clearer goals with actionable steps at every stage.

There are dozens of different ways of incorporating your knowledge of the Law of Attraction into your everyday life, letting your new skills shape your day from morning to night. While that might sound like an overwhelming undertaking, the truth is that simple changes have powerful consequences when you're working with the Law of Attraction. After a few weeks of practicing your new approach, much of it will become second nature.

Visualization Tools

Visualization is a cornerstone of using the Law of Attraction, such as using a manifesting meditation or writing in a gratitude journal. When you spend 10-15 minutes a day building an increasingly detailed image of the life you want to develop in your mind.

Visualization actually extends far beyond these mental pictures and can be practiced in concrete ways every day. This Law of Attraction community can help you to learn and practice writing exercises that help to focus on externalizing goals and making them more real.

These tools and exercises allow the ability to be as creative in this process as you like, and trying out basic skills may inspire you to come up with unique methods that are even more effective.

One of the most important elements of using visualization tools is to find the methods that best maintain constant focus on your objectives.

Some people find different forms of visualization more powerful than others, so we'll help you find the visualization styles that infuse you with the most intense sense of confidence and optimism.

In addition, you'll learn how to combine your new visualization tools with more positive ways of interacting with others, helping you to live and behave as if you have already accomplished your goals.

Affirmations and the Law of Attraction

Affirmations can take the form of internal thoughts or spoken words, but they can also be represented visually. Regardless of how you choose to use them, you can design them to reflect your vision of how you want your life to change.

For example, many people have great success speaking affirming words into the mirror before going to work, or stating "today is going to be a great day" to infuse themselves with positivity upon waking.

When used frequently enough, affirmations can enhance your use of the Law of Attraction by helping to reshape the core beliefs and assumptions that may be holding you back. They promote consistency, optimism, and intense focus on the future you want to create.

Further, visual affirmations are useful ways of reminding yourself to stay connected to positive thoughts throughout the day.

A sticky note on the bathroom cabinet, the fridge, or the front door can keep you in check if your confidence is wavering, and a vision board can be designed to represent your desires and aims in pictorial form.

We'll explain a wide range of ways in which you can use affirmations and teach you how to design them to accurately reflect your underlying goals.

Law of Attraction Exercises

Creative visualization offers a very effective process when it comes to practicing Law of Attraction exercises, in fact they can become your most powerful manifesting weapon when working with the Law of Attraction.

For example, when making this a consistent and daily practice, there are a number of benefits that you can experience when it comes to your physical, mental, and spiritual health.

Law of Attraction creative visualization exercises specifically target negative feelings and help you to work on dismissing them, and ways of stopping self-undermining thoughts before they emerge and spread.

Meanwhile, there are ways to transform your life with living space to better reflect your goals and to inspire an optimistic mindset, and social methods that enhance your communication and help you to spread positivity wherever you go.

As well as offering practical guides to using a wide range of generally applicable exercises that enable you to use the Law of Attraction in your quest to get what you want, we will provide details of more specific exercises that target specific domains.

After all, the exercise you might use in a search for prosperity differs from those that lead you towards romance, and from ones that focus on career goals. We'll also give you suggestions for ways to create your own exercises based on some of the affirmations and visualizations you've already developed.

How to use the law of attraction to build the life of your dreams

The law of attraction isn't a new concept. In fact, it's thousands of years old. Everyone from Buddha to Shakespeare to Walt Disney had something to say about how to use the law of attraction. According to Buddha, "What you think, you become" – the law of attraction can improve your life in ways you've never expected. But what is it exactly, and how can you use it to reach your peak state?

As Walt Disney famously said, "If you can dream it, you can do it." This powerful concept has helped the world's most successful people cultivate certain habits necessary to make their dreams become realities.

They realize that there are concrete steps you can take and habits you can create to learn how to use the law of attraction. You are the architect of your life – it's time to start designing.

Examples of situations using the law of attraction

When asking the question "What is the law of attraction?" most people think of romantic relationships. They're right that manifesting romance and passion is one of the most common uses of the law of attraction, but it is only one piece of the puzzle.

You can use this concept to create a breakthrough in many areas of your life. Want to manifest your dream job, create the body you want, turn a failure into success or change your mindset and stop negative thinking? Learning how to use the law of attraction will help you achieve all of these goals and more.

A loving relationship

Are you stuck in a pattern of relationship roulette? Do your relationships start off with intense passion and romance, only to explode in a dramatic fashion? Or perhaps you find yourself in mediocre partnerships that fizzle after the first few months or weeks, leaving you wondering why you just can't seem to find "the one."

It's easy to blame your partner or circumstances when love is elusive, but it ultimately comes back to you. Are you using the law of attraction to manifest the relationship you truly want?

Do you feel you deserve a healthy relationship or do you feel deep down that no one will ever love you? Are you willing to be vulnerable or do you close yourself off from deep emotional connections? Do you treat finding a partner like a shopping list or are you manifesting true love? When learning how to use the law of attraction correctly, you must ask yourself these questions.

Printed in Great Britain
by Amazon

21898118R00024